GW00383109

Sam, Sam

AND OTHER STORIES

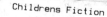

Sam, Sam, sing a song,
Sing a song to me.
Sing of sixteen seagulls
Sipping soda by the sea.

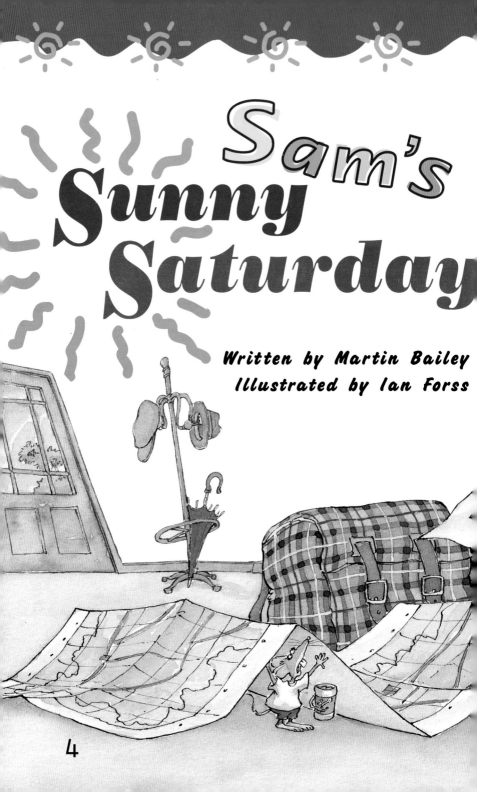

Sam's Sunny Saturday

Written by Martin Bailey
Illustrated by Ian Forss

Sam Hippo woke up.
"Today is a good day
for a swim," he said.
"I will go
to the beach."

7

Sam got his bag.
He put in his towel.
He put in his hat.
He put in
his snack.

"Will you take me
to the beach, please?"
said Sam.

"Too big! Too big!"
said the driver.
"You will have
to take a bus."

"Will you take me
to the beach, please?"
said Sam.

"Too big! Too big!"
said the driver.
"You will have
to take a ferry."

"Will you take me
to the beach, please?"
said Sam.

"Too big! Too big!"
said the driver.
"You will have to swim."

"I will never get
to the beach!"
said Sam.
Then he saw a truck.

the Mover

"Will you take me
to the beach, please?"
said Sam.

"Yes," said the driver.
"I will come
for a swim, too."

Harry
THE
HERMIT CRAB

FOR SALE

Written by Frances Bacon
Illustrated by Philip Webb

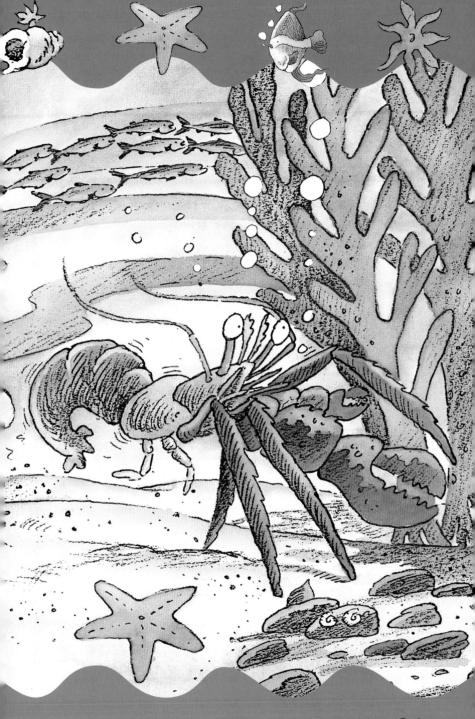

21

Harry the Hermit Crab
was too big
for his shell.

"I will look for a new
home," said Harry.

Harry saw some fish.
"I am looking for a
new home," said Harry.

"No home here!"
said the fish.

Harry saw a big eel.
"I am looking for a
new home," said Harry.

"No home here!"
said the eel.

Harry saw a big
hermit crab.
"I am looking for a
new home," said Harry.

"No home here!"
said the hermit crab.

Harry went on looking for a home.
He saw a tin can.

He went in, but the can was too small.

"I will never find
a home," said Harry.

Then Harry saw
a shell.
It looked big.

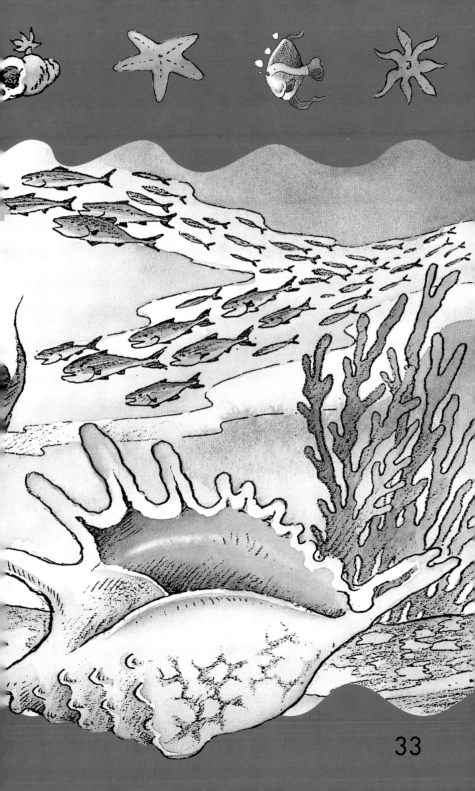

Harry went in.
The shell was just right.

Harry had
a new home.

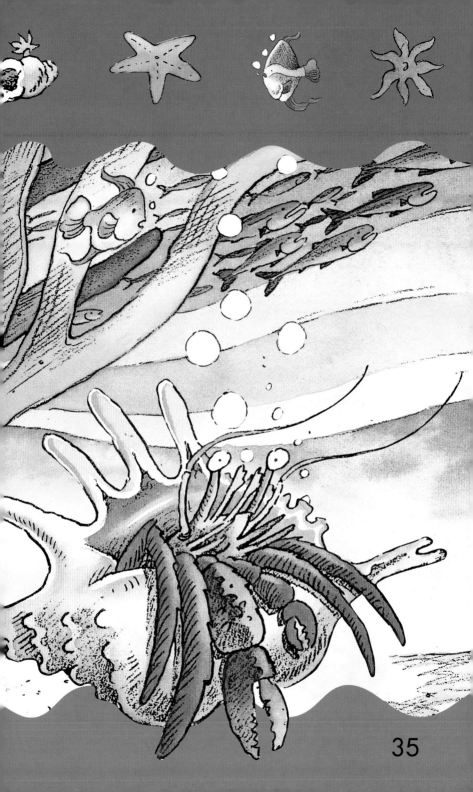

Hippo Hillary

Written by Ruth Corrin
Illustrated by Philip Webb

When Grandpa
goes shopping,
Hillary rides in
the shopping cart.

When Grandpa
goes skating,
Hillary skates
behind him.

When Grandpa
goes golfing,
Hillary goes in
for a swim.

When Grandpa
says, "Bedtime!"
Hillary gets
stuck in the bath.

Sometimes
Grandpa thinks
he should have
a dog for a pet.

But Hillary is happy.
She doesn't mind
that Grandpa isn't
a hippopotamus!